Quick and Easy Knitted Dishcloths:

Beginner to Intermediate Patterns Created in as Little as One Hour!

Tammy Asselin

ABOUT THE AUTHOR

Tammy Asselin grew up in a French Canadian family in Northern Ontario, Canada where knitting, crafting, sewing and home cooking were part of her heritage. Her first childhood memories include images of her mother with hands that were always busy creating. One room of the house was designated as the "sewing room", where all of the treasures used to create could be found. Generations of women in her family gathered in the kitchens of their homes where they worked on individual and group projects, all the while chatting and enjoying one another's company. The children were always welcome to join and it was no wonder that Tammy found herself with a curiosity and a desire to join these women in their camaraderie, resulting in beautiful hand crafted works of art. Whatever the trend of the time; macramé, liquid paint, embroidery, sewing, latch hooking, doll making, scrapbooking or knitting, the results were spectacular. It was however, the love of knitting that remained the constant for her throughout the years.

Although many of those women who first inspired her have since passed away, the tradition of "crafting", and reminiscing of days gone by, lives on in her home.

The Northern Ontario community where she grew up continues to be home. Tammy married a "home town boy" and enjoys the simple, quiet life with her husband and two sons. They enjoy the outdoors and the natural beauty of the geographic area; with fresh air, mountains, trees and an abundance of clean lakes.

WHY YOU SHOULD READ THIS BOOK

Have you had an interest in learning to knit, but didn't know where to get started?

Have you been intimidated by the complicated patterns of difficult projects?

Have you wanted to start with a small project that did not require a large financial investment of purchasing knitting needles, several balls of yarn and pattern books?

Would you like to get started with a small project of something useful and practical?

Are you looking for new patterns for knitted dishcloths?

If you answered "yes" to any of these questions, this book is for you!

In this book, you will find:

- a review of the main knitting stitches and materials used for knitted dishcloths, for new knitters

- a description of the abbreviations for knitting stitches commonly used

- a variety of patterns for completed dishcloths beginning with the most basic of knitting stitches at the beginner level allowing you to work up to intermediate patterns

- PLUS accompanying photo images of each dishcloth to allow you to see the results.

Are you ready to get started? Browse through the patterns and dependent upon your skill level, choose a pattern, get your knitting needles and your yarn and you are ready to go!

QUICK AND EASY KNITTED DISHCLOTHS: BEGINNER TO INTERMEDIATE PATTERNS CREATED IN AS LITTLE AS ONE HOUR!

TABLE OF CONTENTS

INTRODUCTION

Thank you for purchasing this book of my favorite knitted dishcloth patterns. As a long-time knitter, I came upon this trend of knitted dishcloths some 15 years ago. Initially, I could not imagine knitting these beautiful patterned cloths to wash dirty dishes! I was horrified at the thought of ruining the yarn, however, once I began using them, there was no turning back; it is now the only dishcloth I can use.

As an avid knitter, my mother was the first to introduce me to the knitted dishcloths. In the year 2000, my mother experienced an ischemic stroke resulting in left-side paralysis. Although the initial prognosis was complete loss of left limb functioning, she was determined and she was eventually able to walk with the assistance of a cane. However, she never fully regained the use of her left hand, nonetheless, her passion for crafting prevailed! While a patient in a Rehabilitation Centre, she learned to knit with the assistance of a handcrafted aid that held her knitting allowing her to knit with her right hand. My uncle, also a craftsman, quickly constructed a replica of this aid for my mother. It then became her task to knit dishcloths for our family! Following my mom's passing in 2010, I quickly ran out of knitted dishcloths and decided it was time for me to carry on the trend.

I began knitting the basic patterns that were included on the inside of the wrapper of the yarn, but I quickly bored with the same patterns, that I did not especially care for. In search of new patterns, I discovered several handwritten notes of my mother's which included instructions for dishcloths, but I had to visualize the end result as there were no images accompanying these notes. The patterns in this book include several variations and adaptations of my favorites, along with photo images.

This book begins with the easiest level of patterns for beginners with a gradual increase in difficulty to intermediate. New knitters can start with the garter stitch, which is a repeat of knit rows. Stocking stitch is introduced in the second pattern where a combination of knit and purl rows is completed. Next, the knit and purl stitches are alternated creating the seed or moss stitch, as well as the checkerboard or waffle patterns. Additional patterns are variations of these stitches and include yarn overs, knitting two stitches together, knitting below and slipping stitches. Please note that this book is not an instructional book to learn to knit, but does provide patterns, as well as descriptive explanations of stitches for those already familiar with the basics of knitting. An individual who has never picked up a set of knitting needles may find it helpful to consult "how to" or "learn to knit" books, in addition to videos which provide visual demonstrations and instructions.

My personal preference for knitting needles to complete dishcloths is a size 5mm – US 8, to achieve a thicker, larger dishcloth; approximately 9-10" in diameter. I have seen many variations of knitted, but especially crocheted dishcloths, where one ball can achieve two cloths; however, this is not the case for me. The size of knitting needles and size of dishcloth can be adjusted dependent upon your preference. One ball may also go further if you are knitting a simple, basic pattern in comparison to one that is more intricate.   To make the most out of my yarn, I use the remnants to knit 'two colored' dishcloths as in the #2 "Beginner Striped Dishcloth" and #3 "Striped Seed Stitch Dishcloth" or adding stripes to the #8 "Waffle Knit Dishcloth", or any other variations you create.

The time required to complete a dishcloth will also vary according to the pattern and skill level of the knitter. The simplest beginner pattern, with larger needles and an experienced knitter can be accomplished in as little as an hour, whereas a beginner may require a little more time. I have found that I can generally complete a dishcloth in a couple of hours while watching television, as a passenger in the car, as well as while sitting in waiting rooms. Keeping my hands busy, also keeps my hands away from the snacks while sitting in front of the TV!

If you are ready, it's time to get started! I hope you enjoy the patterns for the knitted dishcloths, as well as develop a passion for the craft. When your dishcloth wears out and you feel you can't throw it out, remember they also make great rags!

YARN

There are a wide variety of yarns to choose from, depending on the look of the project you are planning to make, however, the yarn recommended for knitted dishcloths is 100% cotton worsted weight, which is machine washable and dryable. Cotton yarn can be purchased at most department stores, as well as specialty craft stores for approximately $2.00 Canadian a ball or skein.

Cotton yarn is available in a wide variety of colours and styles. For a more intricate pattern, you may choose a solid colour to allow the pattern to be more visible. New knitters may prefer the variegated colours which are more forgiving as mistakes are less noticeable. When choosing yarn, you will find two types of variegated yarn with the second creating a striped result. The #2 Beginner Striped Dishcloth" pattern, is a result of this striped version of the variegated yarn.

KNITTING NEEDLE
CONVERSION CHART

Metric	US	English/UK
2 mm	0	14
2.25 mm	1	13
2.75 mm	2	12
3 mm	N/A	11
3.25 mm	3	10
3.50 mm	4	N/A
3.75 mm	5	9
4 mm	6	8
4.50 mm	7	7
5 mm	8	6
5.50 mm	9	5
6 mm	10	4
6.50 mm	10.5	3
7 mm	N/A	2
7.50 mm	N/A	1
8 mm	11	0
9 mm	13	00
10 mm	15	000
11 mm	17	N/A
19 mm	19	N/A
25 mm	50	N/A

ABBREVIATIONS & INSTRUCTIONS

ABBREVIATIONS

KNITTING TERMINOLOGY –

Knit – K

Purl – P

Yarn over/Yarn forward – YO/ Yfwd

Together – tog

Knit 1 Stitch Below – K1 below

Right Twist – RT

Pass slipped stitch over - PSSO

Stitches – st(s)

Bind off – Cast off

INSTRUCTIONS

Knit 2 stitches together – K2tog – signifies a decrease in stitches and involves inserting the right needle into the front of the first two stitches on the left needle as if to knit, then knitting both of the stitches together at the same time.

Purl 2 stitches together – P2tog – signifies a decrease in stitches while completing a purl stitch. Insert the right needle into the front of the first two stitches on the left needle as if to purl, then purl them together at the same time.

Yarn Forward/Yarn Over – after a knit stitch or before a knit stitch involves bringing the yarn forward between the needles, then back over the top of the right hand needle, so the yarn is now in position to knit the next stitch on the left needle.

Yarn Forward/Yarn Over – after a purl stitch or before a purl stitch involves bringing the yarn forward between the needles, then back over the top of the right hand needle and forward between the needles, so the yarn is now in a position to purl the next stitch on the left needle.

Yarn Forward/Yarn Over – after a purl stitch and before a knit stitch involves bringing the yarn over the right hand needles to the back, so that it is now in a position to knit the next stitch on the left needle.

Slip 1 Stitch – involves transferring 1 stitch from the left needle to the right needle without knitting

Right Twist – involves knitting 2 stitches together, but being careful not to remove the stitches from the left needle, then knitting only the first stitch and now allowing both stitches to drop off the needle.

(*) – work instructions following the * as many more times as indicated in the first instruction

Tension/Gauge – this refers to the finished tension or gauge of the knitted work. Tension is not as important when knitting dishcloths as it will be determined by the size of the knitting needles, as well as your knitting experience. Maintaining a consistent tension will develop with time.

Garter Stitch – a repeat of knit rows

Stocking Stitch – a combination of alternating a knit row, followed by a purl row

Seed Stitch/Moss Stitch – alternating a knit stitch and a purl stitch

1. BASIC GARTER STITCH DISHCLOTH

Materials:

1 Ball of Cotton Yarn

Size 5mm – US 8 Knitting Needles

Skill Level:

Beginner – Very Easy

Instructions:

Cast on 33 stitches.

Knit across all stitches on all rows!

Continue knitting for the entire dishcloth to desired length.

Cast off.

Weave in ends.

*This is an ideal pattern for the first time knitter. Practicing these stitches will help the first time knitter to become comfortable with knit stitches, as well as develop a consistency with tension.

2. BEGINNER STRIPED DISHCLOTH

Materials:

1 Ball Cotton Yarn

Size 5 mm – US 8 Knitting Needles

Skill Level:

Beginner – Very Easy

Instructions:

Cast on 33 stitches.

Knit 4 rows (Garter stitch).

Work 4 rows of Stocking stitch (Knit one row, Purl one row, Knit one row, Purl one row).

Repeat these 8 rows until desired length ending with 4 rows of garter stitch.

Cast off.

Weave in ends.

3. STRIPED SEED STITCH DISHCLOTH

Materials:

1 Ball Cotton Yarn

Size 5 mm – US 8 Knitting Needles

Skill Level:

Beginner

Instructions:

Cast on 33 stitches.

Knit 4 rows (Garter stitch).

Work 3 rows stocking stitch: Purl 1 row. Knit 1 row. Purl 1 row.

Work 3 rows seed stich:

P1, K1, P1 *repeat to end of row.

Work 3 rows stocking stitch.

Work 3 rows seed stich.

Continue working these 6 rows to desired length.

Last 4 rows: Knit.

Cast off.

Weave in ends.

4. SINGLE SEED STITCH DISHCLOTH

Materials:

1 Ball of Cotton Yarn

Size 5 mm - US 8 Knitting Needles

Skill Level:

Beginner

Instructions:

Cast on 33 stitches.

Rows 1-3: Knit across.

Row 4: K3, *(P1, K1), repeat from * to last 4 stitches, P1, K3.

Repeat Row 4 until desired size.

Last 3 rows: Knit.

Cast off.

Weave in ends.

5. DOUBLE SEED STITCH DISHCLOTH (AKA DOUBLE MOSS STITCH AND THE LOST WASHCLOTH)

Materials:

1 Ball of Cotton Yarn

Size 5 mm – US 8 Knitting Needles

Skill Level:

Beginner

Instructions:

Cast on 32 stitches.

Rows 1-3: Knit across.

Row 4: K3, *(K2, P2) repeat from * to last 5 stitches, K5.

Row 5: K3, *(P2, K2) repeat from * to last 5 stitches, P2, K3.

Row 6: Repeat row 5.

Row 7: Repeat row 4.

Repeat rows 4-7, ten times or until desired length.

Last 3 rows: Knit.

Cast off.

Weave in ends.

6. CHECKERBOARD DISHCLOTH

Materials:

1 Ball of Cotton Yarn

Size 5.5 mm – US 9 Knitting Needles

Skill Level:

Beginner

Instructions:

Cast on 30 stitches.

Rows 1- 5: Purl 5, Knit 5 across row.

Rows 6-10: Knit 5, Purl 5 across row.

Repeat Rows 1 – 10 four times.

Repeat Rows 1 – 9.

Cast off in pattern.

Weave in ends.

7. SIMPLE WEAVE DISHCLOTH

Materials:

1 Ball of Cotton Yarn

Size 5 mm – US 8 Knitting Needles

Skill Level:

Beginner

Instructions:

Cast on 35 stitches.

Rows 1-6: Knit across.

Row 7: K7, P1, *(K3, P1) repeat from * across to last 7 stitches, K7.

Row 8: (right side): Knit across.

Row 9: K7, P1, *(K3, P1) repeat from * across to last 7 stitches, K7.

Row 10: Knit across.

Row 11: K5, P1, *(K3, P1) repeat from * across to last 5 stitches, K5.

Row 12: Knit across.

Row 13: K5, P1, *(K3, P1) repeat from * across to last 5 stitches, K5.

Row 14: Knit across.

Repeat rows 7-14 for pattern until dishcloth measures approximately 8" or desired length, from cast on edge, ending by working row 9 or row 13.

Last 6 rows: Knit across.

Cast off.

Weave in ends.

8. WAFFLE KNIT DISHCLOTH

Materials:

1 Ball of Cotton Yarn

Size 5 mm - US 8 Knitting Needles

Skill Level:

Beginner

Instructions:

Cast on 35 stitches.

Knit 3 rows.

Row 1: Knit across (right side).

Row 2: K3, Purl across to last 3 stitches, K3.

Row 3: K3, *(P2, K1) repeat from * to last 5 stitches, P2, K3.

Row 4: K3, *(K2, P1) repeat from * to last 5 stitches, K5.

Repeat 4 row pattern, 10 more times or to desired length.

Knit 4 rows.

Cast off.

Weave in ends.

9. VARIATION OF WAFFLE KNIT DISHCLOTH

Materials:

1 Ball of Cotton Yarn

Size 5 mm - US 8 Knitting Needles

Skill Level:

Beginner

Instructions:

Cast on 32 stitches.

Row 1 and all odd rows: Knit across.

Row 2: Purl 1, Knit 3.

Row 4: Purl 1, Knit 3.

Row 6: Knit 2, *(P1, K3) repeat to last 2 stitches ending with P1, K1.

Row 8: Knit 2, *(P1, K3) repeat to last 2 stitches, ending with P1, K1.

Repeat 8 rows for pattern.

Knit to desired length.

Cast off.

Weave in ends.

10. WAVES DISHCLOTH

Materials:

1 Ball of Cotton Yarn

Size 5 mm – US 8 Knitting Needles

Skill Level:

Intermediate

Instructions:

Cast on 43 stitches.

Row 1:   Knit across (right side).

Row 2: *(Knit 1, Slip 1) repeat across row to last stitch, K1.

Row 3: Knit across.

Row 4: Knit 2, *(Slip 1, Knit 1) repeat to last 3 stitches, Slip 1, K2.

Repeat 4 row pattern until desired length.

Cast off on the right side.

Weave in ends.

*This pattern creates a tight, thicker result which appears as small waves and will require more yarn than most knit dishcloths.

11. 14 POINT STAR DISHCLOTH AKA "ALMOST LOST WASHCLOTH"

Materials:

1 Ball of Cotton Yarn

Size 5 mm – US 8 Knitting Needles

Skill Level:

Intermediate

Instructions:

Cast on 14 stitches.

Row 1: Knit across.

Rows 2 and 3: K4, YO, Knit to last 2 stitches, leaving 2 stitches at end and knitting back across row.

Rows 4 and 5: K4, YO, Knit to last 4 stitches, leaving 4 stitches at end and knitting back across row.

Rows 6 and 7: K4, YO, Knit to last 6 stitches, leaving 6 stitches at end and knitting back across row.

Rows 8 and 9: K4, YO, Knit to last 8 stitches, leaving 8 stitches at end and knitting back across row.

Row 10 and 11: Cast off 4 stitches and knit to end of row, then knit back across row (there should be 14 stitches on the needle).

Repeat this 11 row pattern until you have 14 points.

Leave enough yarn to sew sides together, go around circle and draw circle together. Tie ends in a double knot.

12. EYELET ROWS DISHCLOTH

Materials:

1 Ball of Cotton Yarn

Size 5 mm – US 8 Knitting Needles

Skill Level:

Intermediate

Instructions:

Cast on 40 stitches.

Rows 1-6: Purl across.

Rows 7: P5, *(YO, K2 tog), repeat from * across to last 5 stitches, P5 (right side).

Rows 8-12: Purl across.

Row 13: P5, *(YO, K2 tog), repeat from * across to last 5 stitches, P5.

Repeat rows 8-13 for pattern until dishcloth measures approximately 8" ending with row 13.

Last 6 rows: Purl across.

Cast off all stitches in Purl.

Weave in ends.

13. TEXTURED RIDGES DISHCLOTH

Materials:

1 Ball of Cotton Yarn

Size 5 mm - US 8 Knitting Needles

Skill Level:

Intermediate

Instructions:

Cast on 35 stitches.

Rows 1 – 4: Purl across.

Row 5: P3, K1, *(P2 tog, YO, P1, K1), repeat from * across row to last 3 stitches, P3 (right side).

Row 6: Purl across.

Row 7: P3, K1 below, *(P1, YO, P2 tog, K1 below) repeat from *across to last 3 stitches, P3.

Row 8: Purl across.

Row 9: P3, K1 below, *(P2 tog, YO, P1, K1 below) repeat across from *to last 3 stitches, P3.

Repeat rows 6-9 for pattern until dishcloth measures desired length, ending by working a wrong side row.

Last 4 rows: Purl across.

Cast off all stitches in purl.

Weave in ends.

CONCLUSION

I hope you enjoyed the collection of my favorite patterns in this book! Perhaps you started knitting the first pattern and progressed through all thirteen patterns? Or you selected those that appealed to you and you now have your own favorites? It was my intention to put together a compilation of ten or twelve patterns, but the end result was the "baker's dozen" of lucky 13!

If knitted dishcloths are new for you, hopefully, you enjoy them as much as I do! They are great gifts to share with friends, family, teachers and hostesses; one can never have too many!

Note: Knitted dishcloths absorb most efficiently if you wash them before their first use.

Happy knitting!

REVIEWS

Hopefully, you enjoyed the book and the knitting instructions were clear, photos were helpful and you were successful at completing several dishcloths!

As a self-published author, this is my first attempt at creating a book and it would be greatly appreciated, if you would be willing to provide me with some feedback. I hope to continue to share my creations for different knitting projects, so if you are willing, please leave a review for me at the Amazon page for this book.

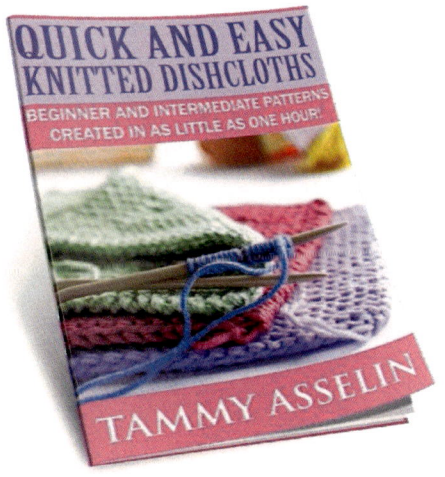

Manufactured by Amazon.ca
Acheson, AB